CHRISTMAS

Vol. 49, No. 8

Publisher, Patricia A. Pingry
Editor, D. Fran Morley
Art Director, Patrick McRae
Copy Editor, Tim Hamling
Contributing Editors, Lansing Christman, Deana Deck, Russ Flint, Pamela Kennedy, Nancy J. Skarmeas, John Slobodnik

ISBN 0-8249-1104-0

IDEALS—Vol. 49, No. 8 December MCMXCII IDEALS (ISSN 0019-137X) is published eight times a year: February, March, May, June, August, September, November, December by IDEALS PUBLISHING CORPORATION, P.O. Box 148000, Nashville, Tenn. 37214. Second-class postage paid at Nashville, Tennessee, and additional mailing offices. Copyright © MCMXCII by IDEALS PUBLISHING CORPORATION. POSTMASTER: Send address changes to Ideals, Post Office Box 148000, Nashville, Tenn. 37214-8000. All rights reserved. Title IDEALS registered U.S. Patent Office.

SINGLE ISSUE—$4.95
ONE-YEAR SUBSCRIPTION—eight consecutive issues as published—$19.95
TWO-YEAR SUBSCRIPTION—sixteen consecutive issues as published—$35.95
Outside U.S.A., add $6.00 per subscription year for postage and handling.

The cover and entire contents of IDEALS are fully protected by copyright and must not be reproduced in any manner whatsoever. Printed and bound in U.S.A.

ACKNOWLEDGMENTS

THE OLD AMAZE from the book *THE GOLDEN SUMMIT* by Grace Noll Crowell. Copyright © 1937 by Harper & Row, Publishers, Inc. Copyright © renewed 1965 by Grace Noll Crowell. Reprinted by permission of HarperCollinsPublishers. SLEIGH BELLS by Edgar A. Guest from *ALL IN A LIFETIME*, copyright ©1938 by The Reilly and Lee Co. Used by permission of the author's estate. CHRISTMAS TOYS from *ROSES IN DECEMBER* by Edna Jaques, copyright © in Canada by Thomas Allen & Son Limited. FOR OUR CHILDREN AT CHRISTMAS from the book *THE PRAYERS OF PETER MARSHALL*, compiled and edited by Catherine Marshall, copyright © 1949, 1950, 1951, 1954, by Catherine Marshall. Renewed 1982. Published by Chosen Books, Fleming H. Revell Company. Used by Permission. GIVING from *PASSING CLOUDS* by Patience Strong, © 1959 by Patience Strong, published by Frederick Muller Limited, London. Reprinted by permission of Rupert Crew Limited, London. Our Sincere Thanks to the following authors whom we were unable to contact: Marie Hunter Dawson for TREE IN WINTER and TO AN OLD CHRISTMAS TREE; William Maloney for IF IT SNOWS; and Ruth B. Field for ON A DARK NIGHT.

Four-color separations by Rayson Films, Inc., Waukesha, Wisconsin

Printing by The Banta Company, Menasha, Wisconsin
Printed on Weyerhauser Lynx.

The paper used in this publication meets the minimum requirements of American National Standard for Information Sciences—Permanence of Paper for Printed Library Materials, ANSI Z39.48-1984.

Unsolicited manuscripts will not be returned without a self-addressed stamped envelope.

Inside Front Cover	Inside Back Cover
Gerald Koser	John Walter

Cover Photo
Jessie Walker Associates

December

Craig E. Sathoff

The coziness around the hearth,
Each brightly glowing ember,
Brings peace and warmth and harbor from
The cold winds of December.

December likes to roar and hiss
And cloak the earth with snow,
And then just settle back and watch
The snowmen as they grow.

It is a time for merriment
And hitching up the sleigh
To gallop through the brittle air
In spirits light and gay.

Hot chocolate and caroling
And gifts we must remember,
The message of our dear Christ's birth
Are all parts of December.

It is a sparkling, tinseled month
That's full of joy and cheer;
It gives a luster that remains
Throughout the coming year.

CHRISTMAS TREE AT DAWN
Bristol, New Hampshire
William Johnson
Johnson's Photography

Merry Christmas

Anonymous

In the rush of the merry morning,
When the red burns through the gray,
And the wintry world lies waiting
For the glory of the day,
Then we hear a fitful rushing
Just without, upon the stair,
See two white phantoms coming,
Catch the gleam of sunny hair.

Are they Christmas fairies stealing
Rows of little socks to fill?
Are they angels floating hither
With their message of goodwill?
What sweet spell are these elves weaving,
As like larks they chirp and sing?
Are these palms of peace from heaven
That these lovely spirits bring?

Rosy feet upon the threshold,
Eager faces peeping through;
With the first red ray of sunshine,
Chanting cherubs come in view.
Mistletoe and gleaming holly,
Symbols of a blessed day,
In their chubby hands they carry,
Streaming all along the way.

Well, we know they never weary
Of this innocent surprise;
Waiting, watching, listening always
With full hearts and tender eyes,
While our little household angels,
White and golden in the sun,
Greet us with the sweet, old welcome—
"Merry Christmas, everyone!"

CHRISTMAS TOYS

Edna Jaques

A little dappled horse, a scarlet ball,
A wooly lamb, a doll with sleeping eyes,
A small white angel for a Christmas tree,
A Christmas stocking with a bulky prize,

Red mittens on a string, a pair of skates,
A toy balloon to drift above the house,
Tinsel to glisten in the candle light
A little, scarlet-coated Mickey Mouse,

A set of dishes for a little girl
With tiny, brier roses here and there,
A locket on a little golden chain,
New patent leather shoes for her to wear.

O crisp December, gay with mistletoe,
Holly and cedar hanging on the door,
Old folks to love, carols to sing in church,
And little children to buy presents for.

Photo Opposite
CHRISTMAS TREE AND ANTIQUE TOYS
Dan Dempster, Photographer

Christmas Cookies
from our Readers

Jam Cookies

2   eggs, separated
1   cup brown sugar
1   cup butter, softened
1   teaspoon vanilla extract
1   teaspoon lemon juice
2   cups flour
    Strawberry or Peach Jam

In a large mixing bowl, combine egg yolks, brown sugar, butter, vanilla extract, and lemon juice. Mix until well blended. Stir in flour. Chill dough for 1 hour, or until firm. Shape rounded teaspoons of dough into walnut-size balls; dip each ball into unbeaten egg white and place on ungreased cookie sheet. Bake at 350° for 10 minutes. Remove from oven and carefully make a depression in the center of each cookie with the underside of a teaspoon. Fill with a ½ teaspoon of jam and return cookies to oven for another 10 minutes. Makes 3 dozen.

Alice Hamling
Aurora, Illinois

Easy Coconut Pecan Cookies

1   box yellow cake mix
1   box coconut pecan frosting mix
2   eggs
½   cup margarine, softened

In a large mixing bowl, combine all ingredients and mix well. Drop by teaspoonfuls onto lightly greased cookie sheet and bake at 350° for 10 minutes. Makes 3 to 4 dozen.

Sharon Sirugo
Sebring, Florida

Cherry Dreams

2   cups sugar
1⅓ cups shortening
4   eggs
4   teaspoons vanilla extract
10 tablespoons juice from Maraschino
    cherries
4   cups flour
1   teaspoon salt
1   teaspoon baking soda
2   teaspoons baking powder
2   cups chopped nuts
4   cups cornflake crumbs
    Maraschino cherries, halved

In a large mixing bowl, cream shortening and sugar. Add eggs, vanilla extract, and juice from cherries and mix well. In a separate bowl, combine flour, salt, baking soda, and baking powder and stir into egg mixture. Add nuts and mix well. Drop by teaspoonfuls into crushed cornflakes and coat well. Place cookie on lightly greased cookie sheet and flatten slightly. Press a cherry half into each cookie. Bake at 350° for 10 minutes or until lightly browned. Makes 6 dozen.

Dory Morley
LaPorte, Indiana

Editor's note: We're looking for a variety of tasty recipes to include in future issues of *Ideals*. If you would like us to consider your favorite recipe, please send a typed copy of the recipe along with your name and address to: *Ideals* Magazine, P.O. Box 140300, Nashville, TN 37214 ATTN: Recipes.

We will pay $10 for each recipe used. Recipes not used will not be returned.

Giving

Patience Strong

At Christmas time, we open up our purses and our hearts.
As the day draws nearer and the dying year departs,
We have the urge to give, to spend as much as we can spare
On making others happy, for goodwill is in the air.

Changes come, yet this old Christian custom never dies.
We say we can't afford it, and we must economize;

PRETTY GIFTS
Dick Luria/FPG, International

But when the time comes round again, we find we can't resist.
For what is Christmas, after all, without a shopping list?

It's not the value of a present. It is not the price.
A blessing will go with it if it means a sacrifice.
Things are so expensive, and one's pockets like a sieve.
But don't suppress the impulse for it's good to want to give.

The pleasure that it brings you will reward you and uplift.
The giver is made richer by the giving of a gift.
What we give to others seems to come back sevenfold.
The copper turns to silver, and the silver turns to gold.

CHRISTMAS CAT
Runk/Schoenberger
Grant Heilman Photography

Read to Me
Art by Russ Flint

Bells of Christmas

Eugene Field

Why do bells of Christmas ring?
Why do little children sing?

Once a lovely shining star,
Seen by shepherds from afar,
Gently moved until its light
Made a manger's cradle bright.

There a darling baby lay
Pillowed soft upon the hay;
And its mother sang and smiled:
"This is Christ, the holy Child!"

Therefore bells for Christmas ring,
Therefore little children sing.

Let the Blizzards Roar

Mildred L. Jarrell

Let blizzards roar complainingly
And blow the snow about,
Let wind-whipped trees
    lash at the sky,
And let cold rains pour out.

I'll dream before a cozy fire,
A favorite book at hand,
Or watch the flames
    and travel off
To strange and foreign lands.

Let the chill of winter bite,
The cold of winter snap,
Let the snow pile
    white and high
In mother nature's lap.

I will wile away the hours
Doing as the heart desires,
Through the winter reminiscing
By a warm and cozy fire.

A Picture of a Village

Loise Pinkerton Fritz

There's a picture of a village
In a valley that I know,
Where the moon is shining brightly
On the newly fallen snow.
Where the air is crisp and frosty
And the night's clear as a bell,
And the evergreens are snow-tipped
On the hills and in the dell.

There's a picture of a village
In a valley that I love,
Where the snow-clad housetops glisten
Like the stars that shine above.
There's a beam that lights the pathway
From one doorstep to the next;
It is the glow of friendliness
In the village I love best.

There's a picture of a village
In a valley dear to me,
And I journey there quite often,
If just in memories.
As I reminisce on places fond
And people sweet to me,
The memories of this village are
The images I see.

Photo Opposite
CHRISTMAS STREET LAMP
Gatlinburg, Tennessee
Adam Jones Photography

Deana Deck

Norfolk Island Pines

Of all the things I love about Christmas, the tree tops the list. I love its piney fragrance, the softness of its lights late at night, the colorful decorations. In fact, until the tree is up, it just isn't the Christmas season as far as I'm concerned. While I can appreciate the traditions involved, all of this has presented me with a dilemma at one time or another.

The problem is that I'm not always home for the holidays. I often travel to celebrate the occasion with far-flung friends or family. Consequently, I often spend hours shopping for a perfect tree, hauling it home, setting it up, and lovingly decorating it, only to leave town a few days later and return home in January just in time to see the last, dry needle hit the floor.

I used to purchase living trees, but there is no place in my yard to plant another one. Besides, they are heavy to move around and need too much care to stay indoors for more than a week without breaking dormancy.

One year, faced with the prospect of wrapping packages, sipping eggnog, and watching favorite Christmas specials without a tree in the background, a solution occurred to me that I had not considered since my college days.

Then, as now, I often left town for the holidays. Like most students, I had little money to spare on something that would only be enjoyed for a short time; but I did have a lot of houseplants, and one was a small Norfolk Island Pine. It was so small, in fact, that it couldn't support lights, so I wound a string of tiny red ones around its basket, tied tiny red bows on the branches, and there I had it—an instant Christmas tree!

The real advantage to these trees is that they grow relatively slowly as long as you do not repot them very frequently. They prefer bright light but can survive in comparatively low-light levels. Keep in mind, however, that the tree is tropical in origin (Norfolk Island is a tiny island in the South Seas, many miles off the eastern shore of Australia), and if you repot them to larger containers, they will keep getting larger. Unless you live in Florida, they will not survive being transplanted to the yard; but if you keep the tree well-watered and rootbound, you will essentially have a slow-growing bonsai plant.

I've experimented a lot with decorating my tree. A sturdy Norfolk Island Pine that is four or five feet tall looks lovely strung with tiny, white lights. Do not use standard size Christmas tree bulbs on a Norfolk Island Pine. Not only are they too heavy, but they are too hot and will dry the tree out.

Since decorating a tiny tree requires few ornaments, you can splurge on really special ones. I have a collection of painted Swedish angels in three sizes. I hang the larger angels at the bottom of the tree and save the smaller ones for the more delicate branches at the top of the tree. One year, I placed large gold balls at the bottom of the tree, mixed medium sized gold and silver balls in the middle, and placed tiny silver balls at the top.

Another year, I discovered that it was easier to have an antique-looking tree with a Norfolk Island Pine. It takes a lot less work to string popcorn and cranberries for a little, container-grown Norfolk Island Pine than for a six-foot spruce! I then bought just a yard each of some very special satin ribbons, tied bows, and quickly had a very unique tree.

Norfolk Island Pines are so easy to decorate that I've come up with many variations. One year, I found some tiny clip-on birds. I clipped several sleek cardinals to the branches, placed a white dove at the top, and hung small pine cones from the boughs. Another year, I made a very special tree with hardly any effort at all. I bought various pastel shades of curling paper ribbon and cut lengths between eight inches and twenty inches. I curled the ribbons with the blade of a pair of scissors and draped the curls over the branches. The curls gently gripped the branches, so it wasn't even necessary to tie them in place. After the holidays, I gathered the ribbons and stored them in a plastic bag for the next year. I must admit, however, that I raided that bag several times over the year for gift wrapping; consequently, I had few curls left for my Christmas tree the next year.

Now that I've solved my Christmas tree dilemma, I am faced with another one. I've come up with so many pretty ways to decorate my Norfolk Island Pine that I often can't choose, but that problem is easy to solve too. Since decorating it is so easy, simply dress your Norfolk Island Pine in ribbons one week, change to an antique look the next, and end up with tiny ornaments on Christmas Eve. You'll never have to worry about your Christmas tree again.

Deana Deck lives in Nashville, Tennessee, where her garden column is a regular feature in The Tennessean.

A Tree in Winter

Marie Hunter Dawson

A tree in winter stands erect and bare,
Stripped of its leaves and black against the sky;
From root to top, from trunk to tiniest branch
Of perfect form, unique in symmetry.

A tree in winter catches falling snow
Along each bough with clumps that drip and freeze,
And in the light of winter's moon, there is
No lovelier strain in Nature's rhapsodies.

A tree in winter bathes in frigid rain
That freezes till a million pendants cling,
Yet all the while the roots are storing sap
To bring the leaves that shelter nests in spring.

Photo Opposite
WINTER ON MOUNT ASHLAND
Oregon
Ed Cooper, Photographer

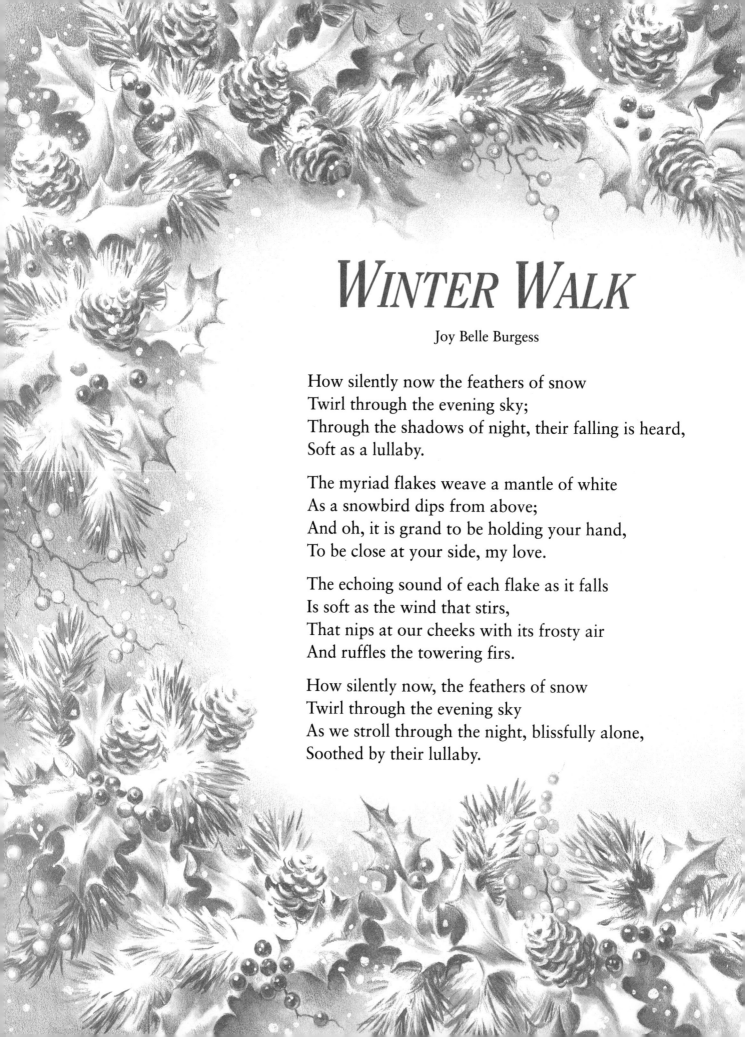

WINTER WALK

Joy Belle Burgess

How silently now the feathers of snow
Twirl through the evening sky;
Through the shadows of night, their falling is heard,
Soft as a lullaby.

The myriad flakes weave a mantle of white
As a snowbird dips from above;
And oh, it is grand to be holding your hand,
To be close at your side, my love.

The echoing sound of each flake as it falls
Is soft as the wind that stirs,
That nips at our cheeks with its frosty air
And ruffles the towering firs.

How silently now, the feathers of snow
Twirl through the evening sky
As we stroll through the night, blissfully alone,
Soothed by their lullaby.

IF IT SNOWS

William Maloney

The world I know, if it snows tonight,
Will be hidden beneath a mantle of white.
The world I know will disappear
And be forgotten until next year.

Icy towers will grow without care
Where once bloomed roses, red and fair;
And crystal cobwebs, silver spun,
Will climb my trellis to dance in the sun.

A snow bush stands where lilacs bloomed,
A drift of white, my peonies entombed,
An empty nest with icicles attached
Where six young wrens once were hatched.

The world I know, if it snows tonight,
Will be covered with a blanket of white,
To rest, asleep, until my God
Awakens it from the sleeping sod.

ON A DARK NIGHT

Ruth B. Field

Long after darkness fell and night
Was wrapped in silence of the snows,
The still moon passed in silver flight,
And glistening crystal pendants hung in rows
Along the eaves. Then suddenly,
Across the dark, a whispered sigh
Became a strange, sweet melody
That filled the quiet earth and sky

POINSETTIAS
G. Ahrens
H. Armstrong Roberts, Inc.

With drifted music, muted, soft,
The sudden woodwinds of the pines,
Dim echoes in elm-choir loft,
And descant of small, brittle vines.

Then, as the wind plucked strange harp strings,
In harmony, like flageolets,
Trees sprinkled notes on night's dark wings,
And icy twigs clicked castanets.
The music of a dark, still night
Can start a medley of small tunes,
While on the hill, against moonlight,
The old firs sound their deep bassoons.

PENNSYLVANIA WINTER MORNING, Larry Lefever, Grant Heilman Photography

Country CHRONICLE
Lansing Christman

Christmas morning is a time of hopes and dreams; it is a time of remembering the beauty and special magic of Christmases past and present. Even though I have seen many Christmases, I still look forward to the season and the celebration of the Christ Child's birth. Some say Christmas is for the young, but I think that no matter how old a person gets to be, there is always something unique to appreciate about Christmas.

I like to rise early on Christmas morning and watch the sky slowly come alive. The pink glow on the eastern horizon slowly grows and throws reaching fingers of red and purple across the brightening sky that herald the rising, golden sun. As the morning goes on, I love to see the contrast between the crisp whiteness of a newly-fallen snow and the myriad shades of green in the pines. These days, I have the patience to watch the day arrive; but as a young lad, I had other things on my mind on Christmas morning.

I remember the joy of youth, the expectancy and the surprise. I remember the Yuletide tree with its ornaments of red and silver and gold; I remember the gifts: new mittens, a book, and a spinning top, the candy cane and orange that

filled my stocking; and I remember the delight on the faces of the grownups as they gathered around the Christmas tree. Even as a child, I could sense the connection that brought us all together. I could feel the rich serenity when all the family was back home again to be part of the holiday.

I have seen Christmas from all sides now. I have experienced the intense joy of a child's Christmas, the warmth of a shared Christmas morning as a young married man, and the pleasure I have now from many years of sweet, old Christmas memories.

My memories are as bright and brilliant as the red of the holly berry on the dooryard tree or the clusters of berries on a black alder brought in from the marsh. They are as glowing as the gleaming lights on the Yuletide tree or the stars on Christmas Eve.

After more than eighty Christmases, I still find awe in all of God's creation—the red of a cardinal against the snow, the blue of a jay, or a rose-breasted grosbeak in the morning sun. I face the Christmas dawn with love and gratitude, just as I lift my eyes to the December stars at night and thank my God for all I have enjoyed.

I look forward to Christmas, not with the unbridled expectancy of youth, but with a sweet serenity. I embrace my old hopes and dreams and relish in my memories—memories as bright as a winter sun and as soft as the glow of moonlight on freshly-fallen snow.

The author of two published books, Lansing Christman has been contributing to Ideals *for almost twenty years. Mr. Christman has also been published in several American, foreign, and braille anthologies. He lives in rural South Carolina.*

Photo Overleaf
MILL IN SNOW
Wayside Mill, Massachusetts
Dianne Dietrich Leis Photography

A SLICE OF LIFE

Edgar A. Guest

Sleigh Bells

In forty years we've changed the world
  and traded many things.
We've banished glowing stoves to gain
  the warmth a furnace brings.
We've polished off discomforts with
  invention's magic art.
We've built the "press the button age"
  when countless motors start,

But thinking of my boyhood days,
  we lost a joy, I'll say,
When faithful horse and cutter
  were forever put away.
For never comes a fall of snow
  but what for them I mourn,
And that strap of tinkling sleigh bells
  we supplanted with a horn!

John Slobodnik

I would not now go back to live
    as once we lived of old,
I'm much too fond of comfort
    to undress in bedrooms cold.
On winter nights I would not care
    to journey to the shed
And carry coal to feed the stove
    before I go to bed.
I'm glad such chores exist no more
    and I am grateful, too,
That wheeling out the ashes
    is a task with which I'm through.
I'm not the kind that loves the past
    and all that's modern scorns.
I merely say that sleigh bells were
    more musical than horns.

We give up youth for mellow age;
    each forward step we take
To reach a joy which lies ahead,
    an old charm we forsake.

We deal and barter through the years
    old customs for the new;
Find easier ways to do the tasks
    once difficult to do,
But sometimes as we move along
    to build the better day,
We learn we've been compelled to throw
    a lovely thing away.
And thinking of my boyhood days
    to this I will be sworn:
Those sleigh bells sang a prettier song
    than any motor horn.

Edgar A. Guest began his illustrious career in 1895 at the age of fourteen when his work first appeared in the Detroit Free Press. *His column was syndicated in over 300 newspapers, and he became known as "The Poet of the People."*

Christmas Day

Garnett Ann Schultz

Do you remember Christmas
Of years so long ago,
The angel on the towering tree,
The candle light aglow?
And do you still recall the dreams
Of Santa Claus and sleigh
And how we'd wake before the dawn
When it was Christmas Day?

Do you remember candy canes,
The mistletoe and pine,
The stockings hung so carefully,
The joyous, happy time,
The Christmas music, soft and low,
The magic organ's sound,
The hushed and quiet Christmas Eve,
The secrets all around?

Do you remember yesterday,
Those lovely dreams of yore,
The hearth place with its faces bright,
The wreath upon the door,
The snow that crunched beneath our feet
And then the warmth of home,
With loving hearts awaiting there
Where gladness was our own?

The gifts and cards, the music gay,
The smell of pumpkin pie,
Cookies in every shape and size,
The snow that piled so high,
The treasures of another day
With peace on earth so dear,
Do you remember all of this
As Christmastime draws near?

Photo Opposite
GAZEBO AT CHRISTMASTIME
New London, New Hampshire
William Johnson
Johnson's Photography

Photograph by Harold M. Lambert

Time Repeating

Nelle Hardgrove

"We came out to borrow a hill," they said,
My son and my grandson, with sled painted red.
And I laughed, full knowing, for a grandson age three,
Snow in the country is the best place to be.

And they soaped the runners of the new Christmas sled,
And away down the hill the laughing child sped.
His dad pulled him up, and back down he went
With our dog chasing, barking, till a full hour was spent.

It seems only yesterday that tall son of mine
Was riding his sled! And isn't it fine
That we are all here and I'm able to see
The joy and the laughter of a grandson age three.

Winter Peace

Ruth H. Underhill

Softly the snowflakes drifted down
Quietly blanketing our peaceful town;
Each tree adorned in shimmering white
Beneath the moon of silvery light.

The rows of houses along each street
Are nestled securely in darkness deep;
The smoke from chimneys in curly form
Assures of people safe and warm.

In the distance a tinkle of silvery bells
As a sleigh skims over the hills;
The gong of a church bell in steeple high
Echoes across the snow-darkened sky.

A portrait of nature in a white wonderland
Perfectly painted by God's great hand.
A snow-capped village 'neath silvery glow:
A magical scene on earth below.

Photo Opposite
COUNTY COURTHOUSE
Hampton County, Iowa
Thomas Hovland
Grant Heilman Photography

ELEANOR ROOSEVELT, 1938. Bettmann Archives

First Lady Keeps
Yule Custom Here

For the eighteenth consecutive year, Mrs. Franklin D. Roosevelt was hostess yesterday at a Christmas party for children in the Womens Trade Union League. . . . The twenty-five young guests have fathers or near relatives who are members of unions affiliated with the league and who are now in the armed forces.

Miss Rose Schneiderman, president of the league, reminded the children that the first party was held in 1924, when Franklin Jr. and John Roosevelt were hosts with their mother. The President, then in private law practice here, also was present at the first party to read Dickens's *Christmas Carol*.

Yesterday, after songs and a greeting to the children and their parents by Mrs. Roosevelt, she gave the signal for Warren Sims, magician, to take over the proceedings.

Donald Hoffman, 8 years old, . . . who had lounged through the carol singing with unfeigned boredom "because we sing too much in school anyway," wiggled in his seat with delight as Mr. Sims came down the aisle and plucked a "magic" gold coin from behind the boy's ear.

Thomas MacSweeney, chosen to assist Mr. Sims, viewed his magic wand with some trepidation until the password was revealed.

"Hokus-pokus is the word," the magician said, "but be careful or you'll make yourself disappear."

Thomas dutifully applied the word only to scarfs, eggs, and rings, with the proper results each time.

The children and parents joined Mrs. Roosevelt in singing "The Star-Spangled Banner" before settling themselves by a large lighted tree in the league's library to sing the carols. Stephen Oleskewich, volunteer violinist, accompanied the singing.

Miss Schneiderman, introducing Mrs. Roosevelt, stressed the common hardships being endured by everyone during the war period.

"The little children like you," she said, "who belong to the Roosevelt boys won't have their daddies home for Christmas either. In this country we all serve on an equal basis."

Mrs. Roosevelt mentioned the possibility of the children's fathers and relatives meeting her sons while in the armed forces.

"Wherever your relatives are on Christmas," she continued, "I'm sure they are all saying Merry Christmas and Happy New Year, even if they can't say it to you, and I'm sure they're all saying that whatever we're able to achieve will make it a more cheerful, happier year for people in all parts of the world."

She then distributed gift packages to each child. In the packages were toys, books, fruits, candy, and a book of war savings stamps with $1 in stamps already pasted in.

The party ended with serving of ice cream, cake, and candy at small tables in the league's dining room.

BELLS ACROSS THE SNOW

Frances Ridley Havergal

O Christmas, merry Christmas!
Has it really come again,
With its memories and greeting,
With its joy and with its pain?
There's a minor in the carol,
And a shadow in the light,
And a spray of cypress twining
With the holly wreath tonight.
And the hush is never broken
By laughter light and low,
As we listen in the starlight
To the bells across the snow.

O Christmas, merry Christmas!
'Tis not so very long
Since other voices blended
With the carol and the song!
If we could but hear them singing
As they are singing now,
If we could but see the radiance
Of the crown on each dear brow,
There would be no sigh to smother,
No hidden tear to flow,
As we listen in the starlight
To the bells across the snow.

O Christmas, happy Christmas,
Sweet herald of good will,
With holy songs of glory
Brings holy gladness still.
For peace and hope may brighten,
And patient love may glow,
As we listen in the starlight
To the bells across the snow.

THE CHRISTMAS SALTBOX
Original Painting by
Linda Nelson Stocks

To an Old Christmas Tree

Marie Hunter Dawson

Come out of the past, old Christmas Tree,
Stand in the corner and let me see
Your snow-white popcorn strung on thread,
Your chains of cranberries shining red,
The bright little candles, twisted and thin,
Clamped to your branches with holders of tin.
Lemon and peppermint sticks and canes,
Homemade presents with all our names,
Clear-colored candy in animal shapes,
Cookies like clowns and jackanapes,
Rattles for babies and tiny dolls,
Pocket-combs, mittens, and popcorn balls.

On the floor are dolls freshly dressed,
The sled newly painted in Grandpa's best,
Crocheted doilies and pillow-shams,
Scarves and kerchiefs with monograms,
Slippers, perfume, and bright quill pens,
Jabots edged in Valenciennes.
Carol singing and conversation,
Special tidbits in celebration,
Old folks happily reminiscing,
Young folks buzzing, dancing, and kissing.

Come out of the past, old Christmas Tree!
Stand in the corner and let me see
All that you hold in memory.

At the Window

One Christmas Eve, when I was five,
Expecting Santa to arrive,
My father waited by my side
For evidence of Santa's ride.

A flash of red, a golden blade
So deeply an impression made
That, though this year I'm thirty-six
And much too old for magic tricks,
The question haunts me to this day—
Could I have really seen that sleigh?

Cynthia Page
Syracuse, New York

Editor's Note:
Readers are invited to submit unpublished, original poetry for possible publication in future issues of *Ideals*. Please send copies only; manuscripts will not be returned. Writers receive $10 for each published submission. Send material to: "Readers' Reflections," Ideals Publishing Corporation, P.O. Box 140300, Nashville, Tennessee 37214-0300.

Christmas Memories

I'm at Grandma's house for Christmas,
Where diamond snow scenes brightly glow;
And in the magic of the season,
Merriest memories overflow.

The tree is green and shapely
In a lovely red-bow trim;
Cute little elves draped in icicles
Smile from the graceful limbs.

The table's adorned with Irish lace,
The center's filled with roses red;
And the chicken dinner's so delicious
With spicy tea and gingerbread.

As grandpa plays his fiddle,
My heart fills with glee;
For it's "Rudolph, the Red-Nosed Reindeer"
He lovingly plays for me.

As Christmas comes, as Christmas goes,
Sleigh bells ring across the snow;
Treasured memories of Grandma's house
Add to Christmas's golden glow.

Ruth Shelton Turner
Parma, Ohio

44

Reflections

A Christmas Remembrance

I remember a Christmas Eve so white with snow,
A memory from long days ago.
My dad and my brother came dragging a tree,
What a good feeling it gave to me!
We listened to records of Chipmunks and Bing
And ate cookies in shapes, then began to sing.

Mom brought out ornaments, old ones and new,
Red ones, green ones, some of blue,
And some that had our names on them too.
We unpacked the garland and tinsel too.
Dad strung the lights, we decked the tree,
And I wondered what Santa soon would bring me.

A few more cookies, then off to bed
For sugar plum fairies to dance in my head.
It seemed I had just fallen off to sleep
When Dad woke me up without a peep.
He said Santa was there, and I had to see.
We snuck down the stairs, but no Santa for me!

An even better sight took hold of me:
Our magically transformed Christmas tree!
Wrapped boxes and toys now covered the floor,
A trail of wonderment from door to door.
Good Old Saint Nick surely had been there
For I felt his presence everywhere.

He gave to me the best gift of all—
A Christmas Remembrance I love to recall.

> Sharon Sutliff Goodin
> Quakertown, Pennsylvania

Little Girl Lost

Oh, magic Christmas, cast a spell
Around our Yuletide tree.
Can you bring back the little girl
Who is lost inside of me?

I long to know again the joy
Of candlelight aglow,
Sweet sugar cookies trimmed in pink,
A doll in calico.

Oh, happy Christmas, memory-filled,
Recapture yesterday,
And help me find the little girl
I lost along the way.

> Ruth J. Wahlberg
> Two Harbors, Minnesota

45

Annie and Willie's Prayer

Sophie P. Snow

*This favorite poem from many years ago is presented again in response to
numerous requests from our readers.*

'Twas the eve before Christmas; goodnight had been said,
And Annie and Willie had crept into bed.
There were tears on their pillows and tears in their eyes,
And each little bosom was heaving with sighs;
For tonight their stern father's command had been given
That they should retire precisely at seven
Instead of at eight; for they troubled him more
With questions unheard of than ever before.

He told them he thought this delusion a sin—
No such thing as Santa Claus ever had been.
And he hoped, after this, he would never more hear
How he scrambled down chimneys with presents each year.

And this was the reason that two little heads
So restlessly tossed on their soft, downy beds.
Eight, nine, and the clock in the steeple tolled ten;
Not a word had been spoken by either till then.
When Willie's sad face from the blanket did peep,
And whispered, "Dear Annie, is you fast asleep?"

"Why, no, brother Willie," a sweet voice replied,
"I've tried in vain, but I can't shut my eyes,
For somehow it makes me so sorry because
Dear Papa said there is no Santa Claus;
Now we know that there is, and it can't be denied,
For he came every year before mamma died.
But then I am thinking that she used to pray,
And God would hear everything mamma would say.
And perhaps she asked him to send Santa Claus here
With the sacks full of presents he brought every year."

"Well, why tan't we pray dest as mamma did then
And ask Him to send him with presents aden?"
"I've been thinking so too." And without a word more,
Four little bare feet bounded out on the floor.
Four little knees the soft carpet pressed,
And two tiny hands were clasped close to each breast.

"Now, Willie, you know we must firmly believe
That the presents we ask for we're sure to receive;
You must wait just as still till I say the 'amen,'
And by that you will know that your turn has come then.

"Dear Jesus, look down on my brother and me,
And grant us the favor we are asking of Thee:
I want a wax dolly, a tea set and ring,
And an ebony work box that shuts with a spring.
Bless papa, dear Jesus, and cause him to see
That Santa Claus loves us far better than he.
Don't let him get fretful and angry again
At dear brother Willie and Annie. Amen."

"Please, Desus, let Santa Taus tum down tonight,
And bring us some presents before it is light.
I want he should div me a nice little sled
With b'ite shiny runners and all painted red;
A box full of tandy, a book and a toy,
Then Desus, I'll be a dood boy. Amen."

Their prayers being ended, they raised up their heads,
And with hearts light and cheerful again sought their beds.
They were soon lost in slumber, both peaceful and deep,
And with fairies in dreamland were roaming in sleep.

Eight, nine, and the little French clock had struck ten,
Ere the father had thought of his children again;
He seems now to hear Annie's suppressed sighs,
And to see the big tears stand in Willie's blue eyes.

"I was harsh with my darlings," he mentally said,
"And should not have sent them so early to bed;
But then, I was troubled, my feelings found vent,
For bank stock today has gone down ten percent.
But of course they've forgotten their troubles ere this,
And that I denied them the thrice-asked-for kiss.
But just to be sure I'll steal up to their door,
For I never spoke harsh to my darlings before."

So saying, he softly ascended the stairs
And arrived at the door to hear both of their prayers.
His Annie's "Bless Papa" draws forth the big tears,
And Willie's grave promise falls sweet on his ears.
"Strange, strange, I'd forgotten," he said with a sigh,
"How I longed when a child to have Christmas draw nigh.
I'll atone for my harshness," he inwardly said,
"By answering their prayers ere I sleep in my bed."

Then he turned to the stairs, and softly went down,
Threw off velvet slippers and silk dressing-gown,
Donned hat, coat, and boots, and was out in the street,
A millionaire facing the cold, driving sleet.

Nor stopped he until he had bought everything,
From a box full of candy to a tiny, gold ring.
Indeed, he kept adding so much to his store
That the various presents outnumbered a score.
Then homeward he turned with his holiday load,
And with Aunt Mary's aid in the nursery was stowed.

Miss dolly was seated beneath a pine tree,
By the side of a table spread out for a tea.
A work box well-filled in the center was laid,
And on it the ring for which Annie had prayed.
A soldier in uniform stood by a sled,
With bright, shining runners, and all painted red.
There were balls, dogs, and horses, books pleasing to see,
And birds of all colors were perched in the tree;
While Santa Claus, laughing, stood up on the top,
As if getting ready more presents to drop.

And as the fond father, the picture surveyed,
He thought for his trouble he had amply been paid;
And he said to himself, as he brushed off a tear,
I'm happier tonight than I've been for a year.
I've enjoyed more true pleasure than ever before,
What care I if bank stock falls ten percent more?
Hereafter I'll make it a rule, I believe,
To have Santa Claus visit us each Christmas Eve.
So thinking, he gently extinguished the light,
Then tripped down the stairs to retire for the night.

As soon as the beams of the bright morning sun
Put the darkness to flight, and the stars, one by one,
Four little blue eyes out of sleep opened wide,
And at the same moment the presents espied.
Then out of their beds they sprang with a bound,
And the very gifts prayed for were all of them found.
They laughed and they cried in their innocent glee
And shouted for papa to come quick and see
What presents old Santa Claus brought in the night,
(Just the things that they wanted) and left before light.

"And now," added Annie, in a voice soft and low,
"You'll believe there's a Santa Claus, papa, I know."
While dear little Willie climbed upon his knee,
Determined no secret between them should be.
And told in soft whispers how Annie had said
That their dear, blessed mamma so long ago dead
Used to kneel down and pray by the side of her chair,
And that God up in heaven had answered her prayer!
"Then we dot up and prayed dust as well as we tould,
And Dod answered our prayers; now wasn't he dood?"

"I should say that He was if He sent you all these,
And knew just what presents my children would please."
(Well, well, let him think so, the dear little elf;
Would be cruel to tell him I did it myself.)

Blind father! Who caused your proud heart to relent;
And the hasty words spoken so soon to repent?
'Twas Lord Jesus who bade you steal softly upstairs,
And made you His agent to answer their prayers.

CRAFTWORKS

An Old-Fashioned Christmas Toy

Materials:

Tracing Paper
1 kitchen towel approximately 18 inches by 30 inches
⅛ yard contrasting fabric
Thread to match
Polyester stuffing
2 ¾-inch buttons
Black embroidery thread
5 inches of ribbon, ⅛ inch wide

Note: Add ½ inch seam allowance to patterns.

Enlarge patterns and cut out of tracing paper. Fold towel in half and pin pattern to double thickness; cut out two pieces. Repeat for ears. For tail, cut a 2-inch x 4-inch strip from towel. For back of ears, transfer ear pattern to contrasting fabric and cut two patterns. Zigzag stitch around edges of each piece to prevent raveling.

For ears, with right sides together and raw edges aligned, stitch front of one ear to back of one ear, leaving opening at top. Clip curves, turn, and press. Slipstitch opening closed. Repeat for other ear. Position one ear on right side of each body piece where indicated and topstitch in place.

For tail, with right sides out, fold tail in half lengthwise. Turn edges under and topstitch in place, leaving both ends open. With raw edges aligned, position tail on one body piece where indicated and pin in place.

For body, with right sides together and raw edges aligned, stitch body pieces together, catching tail in seam and leaving an opening for turning. Clip curves, turn, and stuff. Slipstitch opening closed.

To complete elephant, tie ribbon in a knot around tail, one inch from end. Referring to photograph, ravel end of tail.

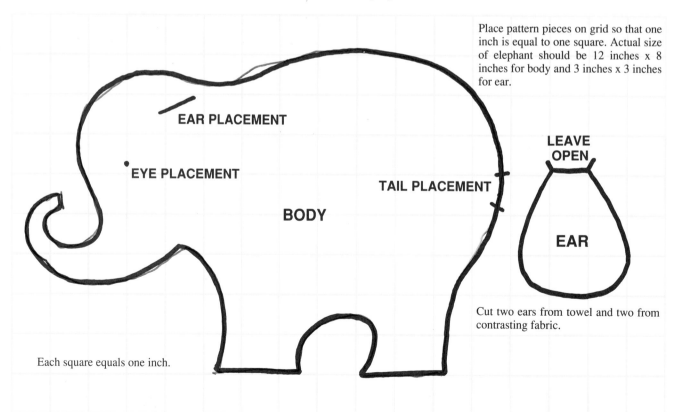

Place pattern pieces on grid so that one inch is equal to one square. Actual size of elephant should be 12 inches x 8 inches for body and 3 inches x 3 inches for ear.

EAR PLACEMENT

EYE PLACEMENT

TAIL PLACEMENT

LEAVE OPEN

BODY

EAR

Each square equals one inch.

Cut two ears from towel and two from contrasting fabric.

Photo Opposite
Gerald Koser, Photographer

COLLECTOR'S CORNER

D. Fran Morley

Collectible Santas

One of the nicer things about a Santa Claus collection is that most everyone has the beginning of one. It would be surprising if the boxes of Christmas ornaments and decorations found in most everyone's attic did not hold at least one representation of Santa Claus.

Probably the most recognized Santa—the jolly, fat fellow in the red, fur-trimmed suit—dates from the 1940s, but versions of Santa Claus, Saint Nick, or Father Christmas go back more than a hundred years. Collectors might choose to begin a collection with new Santas that

are issued seasonally by a variety of companies, or they may wish to look for antique Santa figures, ornaments, and toys.

Some of the more popular antique Santa images were made in Europe from about 1880 until the first World War. Made of pressed cardboard painted and gilded by hand, they are called "Dresdens" because they originated in that German city. New, these figures and ornaments sold for just a few cents, but today a rare Dresden in excellent condition could be worth hundreds of dollars. Not all old Dresdens are that valuable, of course; Dresdens are fairly easy to find, particularly in antique stores in areas of the country that welcomed many German immigrants around the turn of the century.

Also popular with collectors are old tin Santa toys. Like the Dresdens, these sold for just pennies when new; today collectors can expect to pay a hundred dollars or more for toys of this kind in excellent condition. As with other toy or household antiques, the item is considered more valuable if in its original box.

High-quality, blown-glass figures and ornaments from Germany were very popular in the United States right up until World War II. It is still relatively easy to find nice examples of these at reasonable prices. Since German imports were not available during the war, however, several American companies, most notably Corning Glass, also began producing glass ornaments. By the mid-1940s, ornaments made in America were as popular as their old German counterparts. These are probably the ornaments most of us remember from our childhood and can easily be found in antique stores.

Also readily available are old Christmas tree lights in figurative shapes. Less than twenty years after Thomas Edison produced the first light bulb, strings of tree lights became available. In the early part of this century, Germany (and later Japan) produced many figurative light bulbs for Christmas trees. The value of lights from either country is similar, and their appearance is essentially the same. German lights, however, are generally threaded on the bottom of the figure, and lights from Japan are threaded at the top.

Collecting antique Santa ornaments and figures can be fun and profitable, but a good Santa Claus collection does not have to consist of only antiques. Many European companies today are making new ornaments and figures from old patterns and molds, and these are quickly becoming collectibles in their own right. Other companies produce newly-designed Santa Claus figures and ornaments every year in all price ranges. It is certainly possible to begin a nice collection this year with only new Santas.

Someone new to collecting Santa Claus figures and ornaments might think of it as a once-a-year display. Serious collectors, however, often have entire rooms set aside for their collections. Many like to set up special trees—one with only German, hand-blown, glass ornaments or Dresdens, or one with only American-made ornaments and lights—and then rotate their displays. A collection of Santa Claus figures on a shelf or in a case is a nice way to keep the spirit of Christmas throughout the year.

Keep Santa Claus collectibles in mind this year when Christmas decorations are unpacked. There might be the beginning of a wonderful collection just waiting to be discovered.

Bit of Angel

Margaret Rorke

There's a little bit of angel
To be found in every soul,
And it surfaces at Christmas
To promote the season's goal.
It adds sweet notes to the carols,
It betwinkles children's eyes,

And it nimbles flying fingers
As they conjure up surprise.

It's this little bit of angel
That makes Christmas memories sweet
And the story of the Christ Child
Such a pleasure to repeat.
May your little bit of angel
Blend with others in a way
That will bring you peace and promise
And a merry Christmas day.

BITS & PIECES

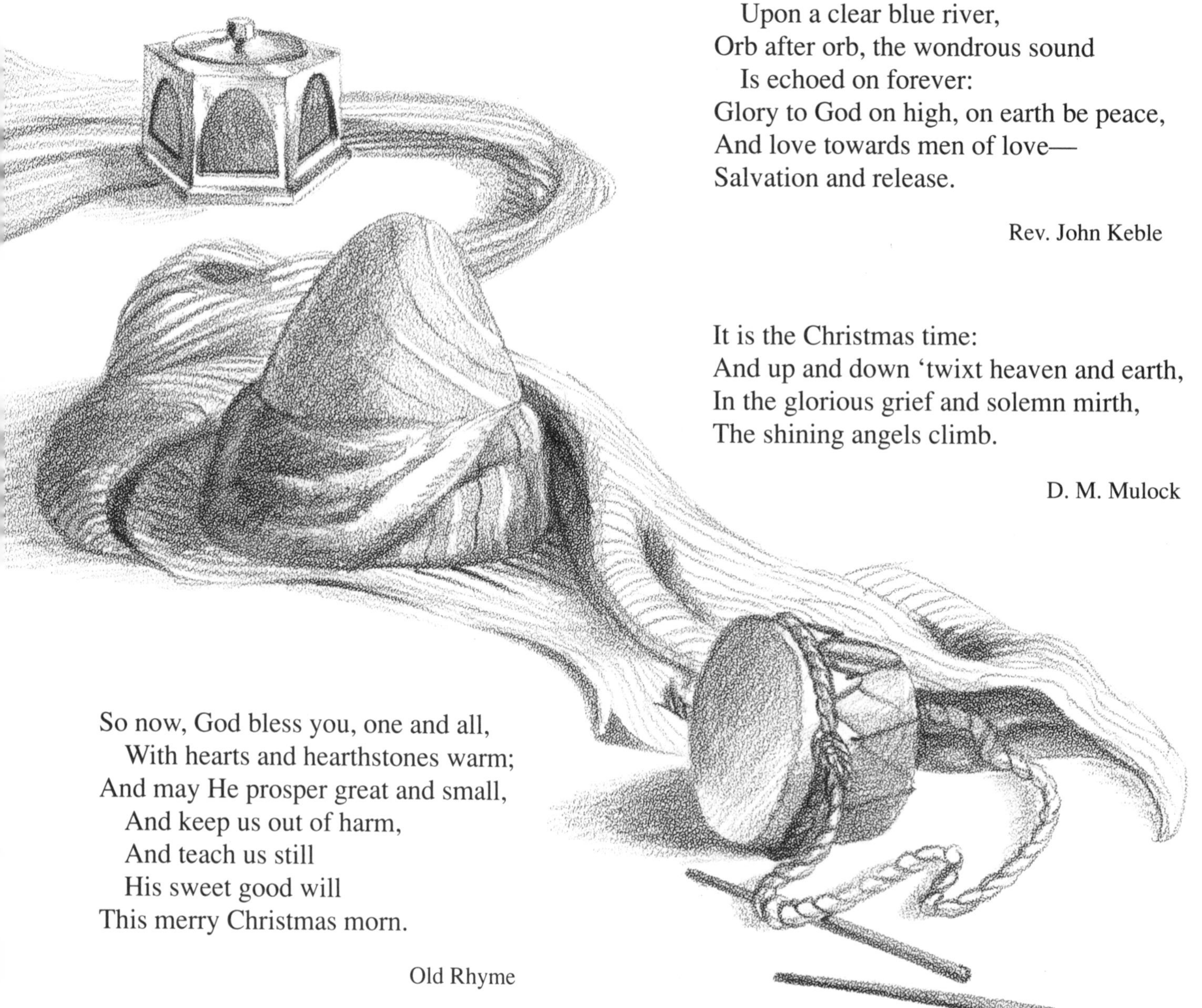

Like circles widening round
  Upon a clear blue river,
Orb after orb, the wondrous sound
  Is echoed on forever:
Glory to God on high, on earth be peace,
And love towards men of love—
Salvation and release.

                    Rev. John Keble

It is the Christmas time:
And up and down 'twixt heaven and earth,
In the glorious grief and solemn mirth,
The shining angels climb.

                    D. M. Mulock

So now, God bless you, one and all,
  With hearts and hearthstones warm;
And may He prosper great and small,
  And keep us out of harm,
  And teach us still
  His sweet good will
This merry Christmas morn.

        Old Rhyme

The time draws near the birth of Christ:
 The moon is hid; the night is still;
The Christmas bells from hill to hill
 Answer each other in the mist.

Alfred, Lord Tennyson

Sound over all waters, reach out from all lands,
The chorus of voices, the clasping of hands;
Sing hymns of the angels when Jesus was born!

John Greenleaf Whittier

The Feet of the humblest may walk in the field
 Where the feet of the Holiest trod,
This, then, is the marvel
 to mortals revealed
When the silvery trumpets
 of Christmas have pealed,
 That mankind are the children of God.

Phillips Brooks

Good news from heaven the angels bring,
Glad tidings to the earth they sing:
To us this day a child is given,
To crown us with the joy of heaven.

Martin Luther

Shepherds at the grange,
 Where the Babe was born,
Sang with many a change,
 Christmas carols until morn.

Henry Wadsworth Longfellow

55

And in the sixth month the angel Gabriel was sent from God unto a city of Galilee, named Nazareth, To a virgin espoused to a man whose name was Joseph, of the house of David; and the virgin's name was Mary. And the angel came in unto her, and said, Hail, thou that art highly favoured, the Lord is with thee: blessed art thou among women.

And the angel said unto her, Fear not, Mary: for thou hast found favour with God. And, behold, thou shalt conceive in thy womb, and bring forth a son, and shalt call his name JESUS.

He shall be great, and shall be called the Son of the Highest: and the Lord God shall give unto him the throne of his father David: And he shall reign over the house of Jacob for ever; and of his kingdom there shall be no end.

Luke 1: 26-28, 30-33

Photo Opposite
THE ANNUNCIATION
Original Artwork by George Hinke

And it came to pass in those days, that there went out a decree from Caesar Augustus, that all the world should be taxed. And all went to be taxed, every one into his own city. And Joseph also went up from Galilee, out of the city of Nazareth, into Judaea, unto the city of David, which is called Bethlehem: (because he was of the house and lineage of David:) To be taxed with Mary his espoused wife, being great with child.

And so it was, that, while they were there, the days were accomplished that she should be delivered. And she brought forth her firstborn son, and wrapped him in swaddling clothes, and laid him in a manger; because there was no room for them in the inn.

Luke 2: 1, 3-7

And there were in the same country shepherds abiding in the field, keeping watch over their flock by night. And, lo, the angel of the Lord came upon them . . . And the angel said unto them, Fear not: for, behold, I bring you good tidings of great joy, which shall be to all people.

For unto you is born this day in the city of David a Saviour, which is Christ the Lord. And this shall be a sign unto you; Ye shall find the babe wrapped in swaddling clothes, lying in a manger.

And it came to pass, as the angels were gone away from them into heaven, the shepherds said one to another, Let us now go even unto Bethlehem and see this thing which is made known unto us.

Luke 2: 8-12, 15

Photo Opposite
THE WORSHIP OF THE SHEPHERDS
Original Artwork by George Hinke

ehold, there came wise men from the east to Jerusalem, Saying, Where is he that is born King of the Jews? for we have seen his star in the east, and are come to worship him.

Then Herod, when he had privily called the wise men. . . . sent them to Bethlehem, and said, Go and search diligently for the young child; and when you have found him, bring me word again, that I may come and worship him also. When they had heard the king, they departed; And when they were come into the house, they saw the young child with Mary his mother, and fell down, and worshipped him: and when they had opened their treasures, they presented unto him gifts; gold, and frankincense, and myrrh. And being warned of God . . . they departed into their own country another way.

Matthew 2: 1-5, 7-12

Photo Opposite
THE VISIT OF THE WISE MEN
Original Artwork by George Hinke

*A*nd when they were departed, behold, the angel of the Lord appeareth to Joseph in a dream, saying, Arise, and take the young child and his mother, and flee into Egypt, and be thou there until I bring thee word: for Herod will seek the young child to destroy him.

When he arose, he took the young child and his mother by night, and departed into Egypt: And was there until the death of Herod: that it might be fulfilled which was spoken of the Lord by the prophet, saying, Out of Egypt have I called my son.

Matthew 2: 13-15

Photo Opposite
THE FLIGHT INTO EGYPT
Original Artwork by George Hinke

THROUGH MY WINDOW
Pamela Kennedy

Joseph's Story

Joseph was a simple man living a quiet life in Nazareth. His carpenter's shop, tucked away on a comfortably busy side street, was filled with the scents and sounds of woodworking. Hammers and chisels, planes and saws hung in order on the walls, and the air gleamed golden as the sawdust rose from Joseph's workbench.

This afternoon, he hummed absently as he planed a piece of lumber for a set of shelves. He was building furniture for his home, the home he would share with his new wife after they were wed in the spring. The curls of pale wood fell to his feet with each firm stroke. Stopping for a moment, he stretched his arms back and glanced at the doorway of the shop.

"Have you been standing there long?" he asked. Mary shook her head and laughed softly at his surprise. He smiled at her. She was tall and slender and lovely. Despite her youth, she possessed maturity and was admired by many in the small town of Nazareth. The older women often

commented that she would be a good wife and would walk in the ways of wisdom described by King Solomon ages ago. Joseph agreed, but he thought more of her beauty and the deep love they would share.

He beckoned her to enter and sit beside him on the bench. He took her hands in his and smiled into her dark eyes. "Why so serious on such a sunny afternoon, my little one? Do you think these shelves won't be deep enough for your bowls and pots?"

"Joseph," she started slowly, "I have something very important to tell you. Something very difficult to explain."

"Ah, you want three shelves now," he teased.

"No, no, it's not about shelves." She looked down at their clasped hands. "Oh Joseph, I am with child."

The words struck him like stones. He dropped her hands as if they had burned his own. "What? How?" he stammered; then, with an explosive burst of realization, "Who? Who is the father?" he demanded.

Her lips trembled, but she raised her face to his and spoke with conviction. "The Spirit of God. He is the Father of my child."

Joseph pushed her away and knocked over the bench as he jumped to his feet. "I am not stupid. I am not a child to be humored with lies, Mary. You mock me. I trusted you, pledged my love to you before witnesses. Now this? You betray it all and then ask me to believe this—this ridiculous story?"

She ran to him and caught his sleeve. "But Joseph, it is true. An angel appeared. He told me I was to be the mother of the Messiah and. . . ."

"Enough!" Joseph bellowed. He picked up a wooden mallet and hurled it across the shop. "Enough I say!"

Mary shielded her face with her hands. Her shoulders shook with sobs.

She looked so alone, so helpless, but Joseph refused to feel pity. "You are a simple peasant girl from Nazareth, not even good enough for a carpenter. What makes you think an angel would ever speak to you?"

Mary raised her tear-filled eyes to his, searching for understanding, but found none there.

"Leave me." He demanded hoarsely. He turned his back to her and did not hear her leave.

The shop that had once seemed filled with golden light was now dark and full of shadows. Joseph grabbed a sturdy plank and slammed it onto the workbench. Long into the night, he pounded and cut, sanded and shaped, working his anger into the wood.

He was tempted to drag her before the Sanhedrin, expose her shame, and condemn her to be stoned. Or perhaps he should divorce her publicly and doom her to the life of an outcast. Part of him wanted to hurt her as she had hurt him, but then he would recall her gentleness and the way her laughter filled a room with warmth. In the end, he knew he loved her too much to make her suffer. He determined to divorce her quietly. Exhausted, he fell into bed and slept.

His dreams were filled with blazing light, and a voice rang through the brightness with piercing clarity: "Joseph, thou son of David, fear not to take unto thee Mary thy wife: for that which is conceived in her is of the Holy Ghost. And she shall bring forth a son, and thou shalt call his name Jesus: for he shall save his people from their sins."

Suddenly, the light vanished, and Joseph awoke in quiet darkness. The words spoken in the dream, however, were as clear as if they had been burned into the timbers overhead.

In the morning, Joseph hurried to the synagogue in a state of wonder. Should he tell of his remarkable dream? If he did, would he be laughed out of the synagogue? Would he be accused of having delusions? Lost in thought, he stood with the others as the Rabbi read from the prophet Isaiah.

"Therefore, the Lord himself shall give you a sign," the Rabbi read, "Behold, a virgin shall conceive and bear a son, and shall call his name Immanuel."

Joseph was stunned. He could hardly believe his ears! Mary's announcement, his anguish, his dream, the prophecy—now he understood. This was not a delusion. It was all part of a divine plan. God had chosen to bless His people; and He had picked an innocent maid and a simple Nazarene carpenter as His instruments.

Joseph was filled with joy. He excused himself from the synagogue and ran to Mary's home to tell her that he believed.

Together, they recounted their individual miracles; and, as they spoke of their wonder, their hearts were joined in fear and faith. At that moment, they had little knowledge of the path before them, but they shared a new confidence in the One who had designed it. They knew, with surety, that He alone could give them the courage to follow where He led.

Pamela Kennedy is a freelance writer of short stories, articles, essays, and children's books. Married to a naval officer and mother of three children, she has made her home on both U.S. coasts and in Hawaii and currently resides in Washington, D.C. She draws her material from her own experiences and memories, adding bits of imagination to create a story or mood.

Christmas Everywhere

Phillips Brooks

Everywhere, everywhere, Christmas tonight!
Christmas in lands of the fir tree and pine,
Christmas in lands of the palm tree and vine,
Christmas where snow peaks stand solemn and white,
Christmas where cornfields lie sunny and bright,
Everywhere, everywhere, Christmas tonight.

Christmas where children are hopeful and gay,
Christmas where old men are patient and gray,
Christmas where peace, like a dove in its flight,
Broods over brave men in the thick of the fight.
Everywhere, everywhere, Christmas tonight.

For the Christ Child who comes is the Master of all,
No palace too great and no cottage too small;
The angels who welcome Him sing from the heights,
"In the City of David, a King in His might."
Everywhere, everywhere, Christmas tonight.

Then let every heart keep its Christmas within,
Christ's pity for sorrow, Christ's hatred of sin,
Christ's care for the weakest, Christ's courage for right,
Christ's dread of the darkness, Christ's love of the light,
Everywhere, everywhere, Christmas tonight.

So the stars of the midnight which compass us round
Shall see a strange glory, and hear a sweet sound,
And cry, "Look, the earth is aflame with delight,
O sons of the morning, rejoice at the sight."
Everywhere, everywhere, Christmas tonight.

Photo Opposite
LUMINARIA CROSS
Tlaquepaque, Sedona, Arizona
Bob & Suzanne Clemenz
Bob Clemenz Photography

LEGENDARY AMERICANS

Nancy J. Skarmeas

Phillips Brooks

Just outside the walls of Boston's striking Trinity Church stands a monument to the man whose words first rang from the church's pulpit, a man who brought comfort, inspiration, and faith to countless parishioners in his more than twenty years of sermons and service at Trinity. That man was Phillips Brooks, rector of Trinity Church, author of the beloved Christmas carol "O Little Town of Bethlehem," Episcopal Bishop of Massachusetts, and one of

the great men of faith in American history.

Phillips Brooks was born in Boston in 1835. He was fascinated by the church from an early age and began to memorize the lyrics to hymns as a schoolboy. He received a bachelor's degree from Harvard in 1855 at the age of twenty and went directly to the Episcopal Seminary in Alexandria, Virginia, where he was ordained to the ministry in 1859. Brooks's first assignment as a minister was at Philadelphia's Church of the Advent. After a brief time, he moved on to Holy Trinity Church, also in Philadelphia, where he began to gain attention for the vigor and intelligence of his preaching, as well as for his exceptional gift of communication. Brooks enlivened Bible passages and gave them meaning for people of his own time. He was beloved by all his congregation, especially the children, who found in their new pastor, not an intimidating authority figure, but a warm, open-hearted man who made religion something they could feel and understand and practice in their everyday lives.

Brooks was so loved in Philadelphia that his parishioners collected money to send him on a trip to the Holy Land, where he retraced the steps of Jesus and his disciples. On this trip, Brooks witnessed Christmas Eve services at the Basilica of Constantine in Bethlehem, an experience that would be the inspiration for his great Christmas carol. Brooks wrote "O Little Town of Bethlehem" in 1868 for the Sunday school children of Holy Trinity Church. The hymn, one of the most popular Christmas carols of all time, is the perfect example of Brooks's skill for bringing all the beauty and mystery of religion directly into the hearts of his parishioners.

In 1869, Brooks left Philadelphia for Boston's Trinity Church. Less than three years later, the church was destroyed in a terrible fire, and a new church was built in its current location in Copley Square. In this spectacular new church, now one of the most beautiful landmarks in all of Boston, Brooks rose to his greatest prominence.

He touched the lives of his congregation from the pulpit—often delivering three sermons a day—and brought his warm enthusiasm and deep faith into their everyday lives.

At two points in his career, Phillips Brooks had the opportunity to rise above the position of rector and assume a role of authority in his church's administration. In 1866, the young preacher was offered the prestigious position of head of the new Episcopal Theological School. He declined. In 1881, he declined a second prestigious position, this time as chaplain at his alma mater, Harvard University. Both positions would have brought Brooks power in the church beyond that of a rector; but Brooks was not tempted, for his rewards came not from fame or power, but from his communication with his congregation.

He was a big, strong, outgoing man; he loved everyday contact with the people who worshiped in his churches. Brooks wanted most of all to bring his passionate faith to these people, not through defining church doctrine, but through communication of his ardent belief that Christianity was the single most powerful force in the world, a force able to transform every individual life and fill everyday with meaning.

Late in his life, Brooks did accept the position of Episcopal Bishop of Massachusetts. He had finally decided to try to work on a larger scale in the hope of reaching a broader audience than he could through sermons in a single church. Unfortunately, it will never be known how much Brooks would have accomplished as Bishop, for he died after only two years at the post. His legacy remains that of a great and inspired preacher. The Saint-Gaudens sculpture that stands outside Trinity Church in Boston as a tribute to the life of Phillips Brooks is physically no match for the size and the grandeur of the church that rises behind it; but in life, Brooks himself filled every inch of the glorious halls of Trinity Church with his warmth, his passion, and his faith.

The Old Amaze

Grace Noll Crowell

These are the things I pray
   the years may leave
Untarnished and untouched
   by dust and blight:
The old amaze, the spell
   of Christmas Eve,
Its rapture and delight,

The breathless wonder
   that the stars awake,
The unfaltering belief
   that a star once led
Three kings a devious way—
   that it still can take
Men to Christ's manger bed.

And, hurrying years,
   in passing let us keep
Some starry-eyed
   expectancy aglow:
The thing that children,
   waking from their sleep
On Christmas morning, know.

And, oh, some little flame
   of eagerness!
Years, leave it lighted
   as you pass, I pray:
A little inner flame
   to lift and bless
All hearts on Christmas day.

TRAVELER'S Diary

Tim Hamling

Trinity Church, Boston

A strong sense of fellowship and community spirit led to the founding of Trinity Church in Boston in 1733. The same devotion which helped the parish relocate to Copley Square following the 1872 fire that destroyed their church has preserved Trinity amid the modern-day skyscrapers rising high above the church's lantern tower in the city's Back Bay area. Throughout its history, Trinity Church has served as an exemplary model of fellowship as its congregation and its rectors have worked together to glorify God.

The Romanesque style and Latin cross plan chosen for the present-day Trinity Church embody the firm, solid tradition on which the church was founded. The graceful, rounded arches over the portals and doors provide a sharp contrast to the meticulously detailed sculpture adorning the church's exterior. Ten large statues of historical Christian leaders—including Abraham; Moses; Saints Matthew, Mark, Luke, and John; and Trinity's own rector Phillips Brooks—are interspersed with friezes depicting scenes from the Bible.

Rising above the nave, apse, and transept arms of the church's main body is the lantern tower, the focal point of Trinity Church. Its yellowish-gray granite adorned with reddish-brown freestone rises over one hundred feet into the air. The tower's mass, however, not its height, is testimony to Trinity's enduring Christian mission.

Trinity's spacious interior is richly adorned with murals and stained glass windows. The elaborately detailed murals are painted directly on the walls and depict figures and scenes from the Bible. The stories of the Journey into Egypt, Samson and the Lion, Jonah and the Whale, and others are told in vivid, narrative detail. In theme they are religious, in style they are artistic, but in their magnificence, the murals are testimony to Trinity congregation's undying love for their parish and their God.

The large stained glass windows in the apse depict seven scenes from Christ's life, including his baptism and resurrection, and are permanent memorials to former rectors and bishops. Other stained glass windows, many that are gifts from parishioners in honor of family and friends, depict scenes from the Bible. Like all of Trinity Church and its history, the interior ornamentation is both inspired and inspiring—an enduring memorial to the devotion of Trinity's congregation and rectors and a living reminder of God's guidance and blessings for His followers.

Despite having a history that dates back over two hundred and fifty years, Trinity Church struggled to be recognized as an Anglican parish in 1733. As the Anglican population in Boston flourished in the early years of the eighteenth century, the city recognized its need for another Anglican parish. A representative of the Bishop of London, however, did not deem the new congregation of Trinity Parish worthy of any financial aid. Consequently, the parish was forced to raise the money for the land and the church building on its own. This hardship, however, proved to be a blessing. Parishioners, by uniting to raise the money for the church they so eagerly desired, formed the early bonds of fellowship that have led the church into the present. Since Trinity Church opened its doors on October 17, 1733, it has relied solely on the blessings of God and the hard work and devotion of its members, never on outside assistance.

In an 1877 sermon, Dr. Phillips Brooks, Trinity's most famous rector and author of "O Little Town of Bethlehem," reflected on the close-knit, familial attitude of Trinity's first congregation. He described an atmosphere where "the people worshiped, and the children grew up with happy love for the Gospel . . . and for the place in which they heard it, and their children followed them, generation after generation, for almost a century." This fellowship and sense of community have existed throughout Trinity's history and can be attributed to the relationship between the rectors, seventeen in all, and the congregations they served with a father's concern and love.

Each rector who presided over Trinity Church helped strengthen the fellowship of the congregation. Their concern for each member, as well as their appeal to individuals from all walks of life, strengthened the sense of community and brotherhood within the parish. Gifts and bequests to Trinity have ensured the church's permanence in Boston, and, most importantly, the sense of community between Trinity's parish and its rectors has strengthened the parish's devotion to God.

WHILE SHEPHERDS WATCHED THEIR FLOCKS BY NIGHT

Nahum Tate

While shepherds watched their flocks by night,
All seated on the ground,
The angel of the Lord came down,
And glory shone around.

"Fear not," said he, for mighty dread
Had seized their troubled mind;
"Glad tidings of great joy I bring
To you and all mankind.

"To you in David's town this day
Is born of David's line
The Saviour, who is Christ the Lord;
And this shall be the sign:

"The heavenly Babe you there shall find
To human view displayed,
All meanly wrapped in swaddling bands
And in a manger laid."

Thus spake the seraph; and forthwith
Appeared a shining throng
Of angels praising God, who thus
Addressed their joyful song:

"All glory be to God on high,
And on the earth be peace;
Good will henceforth from Heaven to men
Begin and never cease."

Photo Opposite
THE BOOK OF MATTHEW
Dan Dempster, Photographer

Suffer the Little Children to Come unto Me

And they brought young children to him, that he should touch them: and his disciples rebuked those that brought them.

But when Jesus saw it, he was much displeased, and said unto them, Suffer the little children to come unto me, and forbid them not: for of such is the kingdom of God.

Verily I say unto you, Whosoever shall not receive the kingdom of God as a little child, he shall not enter therein.

And he took them up in his arms, put his hands upon them, and blessed them.

Mark 10: 13-16

For Our Children at Christmas

Peter Marshall

Lord Jesus, who didst take little children into Thine
arms and laugh and play with them, bless, we pray
Thee, all children at this Christmastide.
As with shining eyes and glad hearts they nod their
heads so wisely at the stories of the angels, and a baby
cradled in the hay at the end of the way of a
wandering star, may their faith and expectation be a
rebuke to our own faithlessness.
Help us to make this season all joy for them,
a time that shall make Thee, Lord Jesus,
even more real to them. Watch tenderly over them
and keep them safe. Grant that they may grow in
health and strength into Christian maturity. May
they turn early to Thee, the Friend of the children,
the Friend of all. We ask in the lovely name of
He who was once a little child.

Amen.

CAPTURE THE MEMORIES OF CHRISTMAS

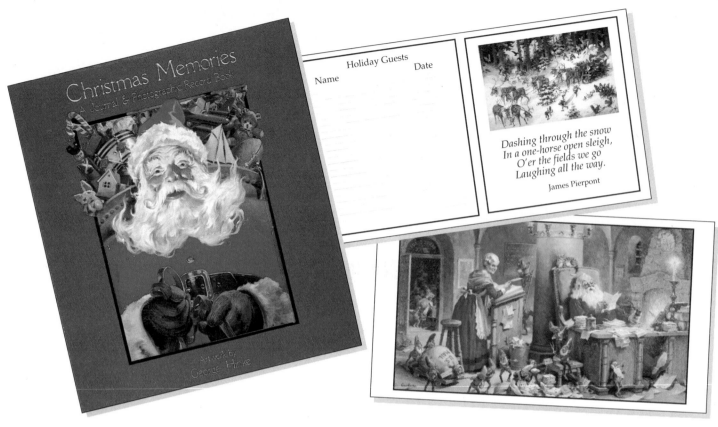

Christmas provides some of the happiest and most touching moments, and memories, of our lives. Families gather and friendships are renewed. The year winds down, and we reflect upon the values of life as we savor the rewards of the year past. Somehow the season always seems too short. Here, however, is an opportunity to capture those memories, to relive those special Christmas gatherings, and to reminisce throughout the year.

A 3-YEAR JOURNAL

This beautifully illustrated journal is the perfect place to capture three years of Christmas memories. This exquisite, cloth-covered book with title stamped in gold offers ample space to record your personal account of the holidays. With 48-pages, this 9- x 10-inch book is printed on heavy art paper which won't yellow or fade with the years. Interspersed throughout the book are quotes and poems which speak of this season of festivity.

SUPERB ILLUSTRATIONS

Throughout, richly detailed paintings of Santa Claus and his reindeer by *Ideals'* beloved artist George Hinke provide a traditional and enduring Christmas experience. From elves stuffing Santa's pack with toys to Santa and Mrs. Claus checking the list of good little boys and girls, this volume is a delight to look at and a joy to use.

IDEAL FOR GIFTS

Christmas Memories makes an especially lovely gift for friends or family members. Order today and begin a Christmas tradition for yourself and a legacy for future generations.